HOW TO BUILD
CONFIDENCE

--- AND ---

WIN
AT LIFE

HOW TO BUILD CONFIDENCE

CONFIDENCE

— AND —

WIN

AT LIFE

CORY GREGORY

To my immediate family, who has always believed in me.

Mom, you are the most caring and strongest person I know.

Frank and Patricia Boone for always being there for us.

RIP Papa for being the example of the man
I wanted to be when I grew up.

Dave Gregory, RIP. I miss you dearly every day.

My stepdad, Randy Thompson. You helped me so much.

My sister, Bettina. We've been through it sis.
I love you and I'm super proud of you.

Rachael you are the love of my life.
None of this would ever be possible without you.

To my kids Alex, Madelyn and Anden.
I want you to know I love you guys so much, and I created
this book with you guys in mind. I want you to live out
your dreams and know that anything is possible.

A special thanks to my editor Daniel Walter and
the graphic designer Cole Susac for bringing the fire
and making this book a reality.

Lastly, to all the real ones that support what we do at Max Effort
Muscle, Old School Gym, and CoryG Fitness.

CONTENTS

OVERVIEW

T his book is meant to help anyone who wants more for themselves and those who don't want overthinking to be an obstacle to going after their dreams.

This book is about believing it is possible.

It takes a strong, daily strategy to instill confidence at this level. It's imperative to be able to manage the ups-and-downs while moving forward. Continually doing so will show you what's possible, and then you're left to execute.

I've lived these thoughts, put in the work, and have seen the other side that I never thought was possible. I went from shoveling coal 600-feet underground to smoking stogies with my idol, Arnold Schwarzenegger, on his back porch at Christmastime as his business partner.

Life can be incredible, but your strategy has to be real. It has to be consistent. And, it has to be intentional. You must have the appropriate plan in place in order to execute. I can be that example for you, and I can show you a roadmap of how to implement the same plan in your life.

Let's get started.

INTRODUCTION

I WAS TIRED OF living paycheck to paycheck. I was tired of watching the people I love most hate their jobs, and I was tired of constantly being let down. I absolutely hated thinking that winning the lottery was our best hope for change.

Believe me, it wasn't.

At the age of 15, I was fed up with my financial and living situation. At about the same time, I fell in love with lifting weights. The obsession of building confidence through the iron, coupled with learning the original teachings of Arnold from books & magazines, changed everything for me. The funny thing is this was all before the arrival of this new thing called the internet.

I wanted to be featured on the cover of magazines and to be able to change my family for generations to come.

How does one do that? Confidence.

How does one from humble beginnings take risks and win? Confidence.

How does one believe that they can open a gym for $5,000 with zero direction at age 20? Confidence.

How can someone close the business deal of a lifetime with The G.O.A.T. of the industry to create a new supplement line? Confidence.

I wouldn't have been able to achieve any of these things if I was a fake or fraud. This is real. This is what I worked for, and this is what you need to hear with hopes to help you build yours. I don't have a 14-day course, but a life plan of continuous operation that I'd like to share with you. If you go all-in, you'll never be the same. I guarantee it.

Will this be easy? Absolutely not. But, this will change you forever and once you experience it, you know. I have always learned through actions and through stories of others and that is how I will teach you. The impact of others is the sauce that many don't realize they need.

I started this process to change my family forever. That, and that alone, is my definitive purpose. Now, my personal mission has spilled into the real world and my professional career.

With so many people now following me, I don't take this lightly. I take it as a responsibility to teach and make sure my material is out there to help. As crazy as I sound sometimes (even to myself), I know it helps.

I'm going to lead you through how and why I am who I am today and what I do each day to continue to build myself up. I'm not done with this process - not even close - and neither are you!

Let's get started on the road to building more confident versions of ourselves.

CHAPTER ONE

THE TRAILER, LOTTERY & COAL MINE

T HE TRAILER, THE lottery, and the coal mine have played a massive role with why I want to change future family generations. Let's dive into my past that has shaped me into the man I am today and laid the foundation for every bit of success I've had.

The Lottery

Growing up in rural Ohio, I remember the lottery being extremely popular for some reason. Maybe it still is. My father constantly played the *Pick Four*, *Box It,* and *Do It Straight.* A portion of his money was literally allocated for each day, week, and month on lottery tickets.

My father's regular lottery play allowed us to imagine a better life, and our hopes went through the roof. We thought that when those numbers were called, all of our problems would magically dissolve and we'd be in a more fortunate position in life.

There were times he was working in the coal mine and everything was going great. However, the memories that stick in my mind are the strikes, the constant financial strain, and the different side jobs just to make ends meet. Although he wasn't able to clear life's major hurdles, I give him props for always trying new things.

From what I remember, my father thought he was going to beat the system. He played the numbers over and over, and even kept track of them in a book. He spent more time attempting to win as a gambler than he did on his attempt to be a successful businessman.

This playbook created a false hope that ultimately caused me to despise the lottery. I hated the fact that I was waiting on something I wasn't able to control through hard work, perseverance, and proper education.

I couldn't make it happen.

It was a perpetual cycle of building up hope, only to be followed by the ultimate letdown. Subscribing to the lottery as the solution to your problems simply isn't reality, and endorsing this idea is a one-way ticket to developing a serious gambling problem. I wasn't fully aware of what was really happening at the time, but I now realize the problems this mindset can create.

My father passed away years ago, and losing him is still one of the worst days of my life. There were loose ends I wish I could have changed and lost conversations that needed to be had. As I get older, I wish I could talk to him now as a more developed individual. He was a very nice person who lost his way with a few things in life. To be straight, the stories of him as he got older were hard to hear, but still showed progress that he was trying harder the second time.

My father died in a single-car accident coming home from work. This traumatic event changed my life forever and gave me a daily perspective I'll never forget. I would change nothing about the way I was raised because I wouldn't be me without these experiences. The experiences from my childhood and upbringing have made me stronger and more insightful.

I do know that he loved my sister and I. I wish I could paint him in a perfect light, but I can't. I wish that it could have ended differently, but it didn't. So, we keep it moving forward with a heavy heart.

The Trailer

My parents divorced when I was 11 years old. After my dad left, we struggled to make ends meet. My mom worked as many jobs as possible to make sure we had food on the table, and even my grandparents chipped in when they were able.

Once I hit the sixth grade and we moved in with my grandparents, my worldview began to shift dramatically. This was the time when I was first introduced to lifting weights.

The man responsible was the man who would become my idol: my grandfather Frank Boone.

When he came home from his construction job for the day, we would head straight for the weights. He explained to me that lifting would increase my confidence, increase my strength for sports, and the girls would like it too. I said sign me up!

I deeply admire and idolize my grandpa still to this day. He was big, strong, tough, and a man of his word. As I write this book in 2021, he's 93 years old and in the hospital. He's exactly who I wanted to be growing up and an all-around great human being.

Living with my grandparents over the course of a year helped to teach me the value of consistency with lifting weights. My first taste of progress was a few months in when I started to see a little delt cut while doing upright rows.

That's all it took. My confidence soared, and I was 100% hooked on the feeling of lifting weights and making myself better.

As an added bonus, my new obsession allowed me to spend a great deal of time with the man who has served as my main father figure my entire life. No matter if we were lifting weights or golfing, seeing my grandfather on a regular basis was extremely important to me.

Looking back, it's hard to understate how large of an impact this one-year window of time would have on my life. I learned the value of being consistent, how to increase my confidence, and how to believe in myself. My grandfather helped to instill the confidence to believe I could do whatever I wanted to do. Always having him in my corner helped me on the road to success.

Back on Our Feet

As we made our way back to independence, my mom began adjusting to being a single parent. The one place we were able to afford was a mile away on the front of a nice, quiet, country road. There were some nice houses towards the end of the road, but our future home was a 1970's trailer at the front.

Let me paint you a picture...

I'm not going to sugarcoat it. It was rough. The trailer was old and falling apart. The roof sagged so badly that I would take a broomstick to push off the excess snow and water from the roof. At 5'11, I could literally touch the ceiling with the top of my head. It got so bad that I had to get help from my Uncle Mike - who works in construction - to help install a makeshift brace just to hold the ceiling up.

The rent due for our trailer was $150 per month, and I know for a fact that this payment was not easily made each time. My mother was a waitress, worked side jobs, and did anything she could do to make sure we were taken care of. Sure, we didn't have designer shit, but we didn't go without.

I vividly remember the hardship and stress my mom endured, tirelessly trying to make ends meet. She was always struggling, persevering, and working hard - all while raising my sister Bettina and me.

I always tell my mom to not be upset when she reads stuff like this because these are the experiences that have shaped me to be the animal I am today. She is truly a remarkable woman, and I am so proud of her and my sister. We made it, even when things sometimes seemed bleak.

Finding Inspiration

I was embarrassed to live in a trailer. All my friends that I played sports with had parents that worked at the sawmill, coal mine, school, or had their own business. One of the families around us, the Dorsey's, owned a grocery store. They had a nice house, a multiple-car garage and a pool. Having the Dorsey's as a template for how I wanted my life to look helped me greatly.

Cliff and Cindy Dorsey, their son Josh, and his two sisters were such a model family for me to look up to. Cliff and Cindy did a great job of being an example for me even though they were unaware. Josh has grown up to be an entrepreneur himself, building a successful online chiropractic business.

All I had to do was ride my bike down to their house to see it in real time. They had the big screen TV, Nintendo, pool, and the four-wheelers. They were able to afford these luxuries because they took on entrepreneurial risk. For me, this revealed the door of possibilities, and that door hasn't closed since. If I had never been exposed to this environment, I would have never even imagined that it would be possible for me to have all those things as an adult.

And so, my preliminary model of entrepreneurship was born. I could see where I wanted to go, and I had a model to start with. Having the opportunity to look under the hood to see how people operate makes all the difference. Another major key was that Cliff and his brother Kenny were also former coal miners. They showed me what was possible, and that my dreams were realistic if I worked hard.

My First Car

I realize now that it was an immature way to think, but I was embarrassed to have my girlfriends over because of the cars I had. My first car was only $300. My second car was just $500.

My second car was a Plymouth Horizon with multiple-colored doors and broken door handles. The only handle that worked was the passenger rear door. When I had to get gas, I would try so hard to keep the door from latching so that I didn't have to climb through the passenger rear door to get into the driver's seat and have everyone look at me.

I couldn't stand the feeling of being *less than basic*. I just wanted my door handles to work. For the ceiling to not be caving in.

To be *normal*. I just wanted to be in the same ballpark as the people I operated with.

There are *always* people that have it worse than you do. Irregular access to food, drug addictions, and physical abuse plague many families. In my case, I witnessed a gambling habit and financial strain between my parents. Hardship revealed to me the significance of consistency and perseverance, while helping me gain the clarity I needed to see that I wanted something more out of my life.

Hard Work

Growing up, I worked my ass off doing farm jobs. On the basketball court I dedicated countless hours to becoming a better player, even though it didn't amount to as much as I hoped. I applied that same relentless work ethic, plus some, to studying lifting weights. I fell in love with the feeling of lifting, and *it changed me forever.*

I vividly remember reading muscle magazines and lifting cement weights in my trailer. I didn't even have the real thing, but that's where the dreams began. The dreams of having muscles, abs, being more confident, getting the girls, and getting out of my situation.

At that moment, I knew I was not only meant to do big things, but that I was going to do whatever it took to make those big things happen.

I identified at a deep level with the aspirational hip hop lyrics I listened to regularly.

The come-up, the opportunity, and emerging from unfortunate circumstances.

Advancing from the lower-income bracket, loving your job, and wanting something more for yourself.

Wanting to improve your financial situation, wanting to learn how to produce more money, and wanting to learn how to run a successful business.

These are some of the thoughts that ran through my mind on repeat. Knowing that there was another way was something I couldn't get out of my mind.

I didn't yet know how I was going to do it, but I knew that I was going to be different. I knew that the confidence I had in myself would only grow, and I was willing to do whatever it took to change future generations of my family. I was going to be the last person with the name Gregory to live in a trailer or have that lifestyle. I was going to create generational change.

Throughout history, numerous people have taken it upon themselves to change their circumstances because they were fed up. I hit that very same point back in the trailer, and I never looked back.

Coal Miner

My mom remarried when I was 18 years old to a man named Randy Thompson. Randy worked in the coal mines for 40 years and has served as another strong father figure in my life by showing me the value of hard work.

Starting out, we didn't get along great because I was into partying and messing around, but we did have two big things in common: We both loved lifting weights, and we both loved my mom. Our relationship grew stronger over the years, eventually leading to him being able to identify and understand my deep desire to do something wildly different with my life.

After high school graduation, I landed my first job slinging lumber at Denoon Lumber. A powerful family in the area built a business around cutting wood beams, then selling them to the coal mines. These wood beams helped support the ceiling of the mines so they wouldn't cave in.

This man was able to build a multi-million-dollar business selling lumber all over the world, all the while employing almost an entire town. Seeing a business of this magnitude up close had a huge impact on me.

My routine at the time was community college from 8am-noon, then over to the lumberyard to stack lumber from 1-10pm. I did that routine for about a year, and straight up, I hated my life doing this kind of work. The schedule and money I made just weren't cutting it, and the lifestyle was making me miserable. I learned a lot at Denoon Lumber, and I appreciate all the men that helped me grow up. I just knew that $7 an hour, 10 hours a day, wasn't for me. I knew that I couldn't do a job that I didn't love and wouldn't help me change my family's circumstances.

And that's when Randy told me that he could get me a job in the coal mine.

Being 600 feet underground and up to eight miles in, working in a coal mine qualifies as one of the most dangerous jobs out there. The base rate was $14 per hour, and overtime was $21 per hour. At the time, there was such a high demand for workers that I was able to pick up as many overtime hours as I could physically handle. And, we all know that I can handle a lot.

This was also the exact time that many of my friends were leaving for Columbus to start college. Although a four-year degree wasn't something I was interested in, I eventually stumbled across Columbus State's one-year Exercise Specialist Certification. This particular program essentially helped you to achieve elite personal trainer status.

I now had a path, I saw the goal, and I knew what I needed to do.

In the coal mine I was racking up 60-90 hour workweeks over four months. I then put in two more months of work underground for a grand total of six months in the mine.

Before I left the Ohio Valley, I had more than $20,000 saved. I had worked my ass off for that money, and I knew I was going to make shit happen with it.

What I Learned as a Coal Miner

Being a coal miner is just straight up tough. You become a man real quick doing this type of work. You have to get up with the intention to work your ass off for as long as physically possible. I was forced to prepare my mind for some of the shittiest working conditions you can ever imagine.

Shifts started at 5 or 6am, and you didn't quit until the job was done. I remember working 16 and 20-hour shifts. Sometimes I would work 14 hours, come out, then go right back in for another 14 hours. My work ethic had officially reached a maniacal level because I had a goal, a timeframe, and a destination. The money I made from mining was my ticket out.

The ceiling was 38-42 inches high. I shoveled on my knees for 16 hours onto a belt that was so loud I couldn't hear myself think. Water leaked from overhead onto a muddy floor, while my back scraped the ceiling, and I shoveled coal onto the beltline all day long. When you work a job this hard and extreme for 16 hours, *everything else feels easy*. Enduring the same work conditions of past family generations changed everything for me.

From time to time, people throw hate at me saying that I can't really call myself a coal miner because I only did it for six months. Well, if you've never been 600 feet underground and rode seven miles into the earth to start your shift, you have no business here.

It was a 45-minute ride *underground* to simply get to my worksite. You don't think that's fucking scary? If the ceiling collapses, that's it. No one is going to be able to get you.

It forced me to fully understand and respect the danger of this work each and every day. It's also why I have mad love for coal miners. They put their lives on the line every day to make sure the lights are on. I take pride in having been a coal miner. I know where I came from. I know how I got here, and I'm proud to have four generations of coal miners coursing through my veins.

Go Time

I put in the work. I saved up the money. Now, it was go time.

It was time to put everything I had learned up to this point to the test. The trailer, the lottery, and the coal mine gave me the juice to want more for my life, and I was about to embark on the journey to make it all happen.

When I was initially writing this I talked about my grandpa being in the hospital. He passed away shortly after I wrote this. COVID made seeing him extremely difficult, but fortunately, I was able to see him on what they call the "rally day." The "rally day" is the day before someone passes where the person experiences enhanced cognitive awareness and function for a short period of time.

This man meant absolutely everything to me. We were able to watch golf together in the hospital, he told me how he liked my shirt, and he told me that he loved me. All as if nothing was wrong. I gave him a big hug and thought to myself, "Man, he seems fine. This old man is going to come out of this." A couple hours later he passed away. Selfishly, I want to believe that he waited on me because he had already seen most everyone else.

My grandpa is my idol and I miss him dearly. I love you Papa.

CHAPTER TWO

EMBRACE THE RAGE

E MBRACING THE RAGE took me to another level. A lot of things in my life made me angry, and I learned how to embrace that inner feeling to bring about positive change. All the things that I'm teaching you in this book are building confidence based around the process of change. You have to decide that you want to dig deep - part of that was you deciding to read this book. Now you need to ask yourself this question:

Why do you want the change?

I wanted to change because I was tired of being the kid that didn't have the financial foundation and setup that his friends had. I was tired of being the kid that felt like we couldn't connect the dots financially and was always living paycheck to paycheck. I was tired of being the kid that watched my parents fight and my dad being on strike at work. *Financial IQ* or the concept of saving and making money wasn't a topic of discussion, nor was it understood. I was tired of feeling like I was worth less than others because I lived in a trailer and because I didn't have the fresh gear to wear. *I was tired of the entire situation.*

Was I starving? Absolutely not, but we probably should have been on government assistance. My mom might've been too proud to do that, but the reality is that we probably would've been better off if we did. The struggle from check to check was real. My mom was a waitress, and my dad wasn't around much. I was tired of the never ending struggle, and I knew there had to be a better way.

On top of this, I would consider myself a less than great athlete. I worked my ass off, but I wasn't able to always translate that onto the court or onto the field. I really believed that my way out of my situation was going to be a scholarship, but in reality, I wasn't even being recruited. I started thinking to myself, "What am I going to do?"

Dig Deep

I started digging deeper and deeper into the weeds of my mind to confront and embrace these feelings. I was flat out sick and tired of it. These feelings and these things were meaningful, upsetting, and hurtful.

I was upset that my parents were split up and that my dad left when I was 11 years old.

I was upset that he didn't spend much time with me and that he spent much of his money on the lottery.

I was upset that my mom struggled to the point of barely being able to pay the rent. She worked like crazy and was probably beaten to a pulp.

I was upset that I had to buy the dope shit at my friend's yard sale two years after he wore it because I couldn't afford it.

I mean, I wanted to be the guy with the house with the pool and the dope rides and somebody in my community that people looked up to. I wanted to understand finances. I wanted to create a legacy that changed my family's future generations. I wanted all of those things. *Embracing my desire for all of these things helped shape me to be different.*

It's a painful process, and for some people, the pain is too great. The pain paralyzes them, and they're stuck. I urge you to dive deep, confront the pain, and use it to get better. I used this very process to change my life for the better.

What Sticks Out?

All of the things that I'm teaching you in this book are going to help you, but you have to embrace the items that mean the most to you. For me, one of those things is the trailer that I grew up on. I think back and remember it being so old the roof would almost fall in when it snowed. I remember having to work with my uncle to build a makeshift brace just to hold the ceiling up. And even after that, I'd have to go outside and push the snow off the roof so the motherfucker wouldn't collapse.

When I think of that, I think to myself, are you fucking kidding me? It was just the reality of the situation. My bedroom was smaller than a walk-in closet. My car growing up had one door handle. I was climbing through the back door at the gas station on the passenger side, hoping that no one saw me.

All that shit motivated me back then and it still motivates me today. I embraced that rage a long time ago of hating my situation and forcing myself to do the things I needed to do to get out of there and build a better life for my family.

What Drives You?

Man, fuck all that. That's exactly how I would feel when I think about those things, and that's what helped drive me to another level. One of those things that I dealt with and struggled with was that my dad was a bit of a loner and never engaged much with me. Part of that drive gets internalized and you become biologically connected to it. I know this now because I have certain triggers from this experience with my father.

For example, when my kids ask me to do certain things that my dad used to say no to, I *always* say yes. Even when I don't want to, I *always* say yes. This is something I wanted badly from my dad, so I knew this was something I wanted to change.

Zoom In

Digging into what drives you is the key. That's where much of the difference is. Zooming in on these things can be painful because it's these things that shaped you as a person. Sometimes you felt like there was no possible way out or way to change your situation. At the same time, it's those experiences that can drive you to another level if you learn how to harness them right.

Resources seemed slim at the time, especially with the internet not being around.

How do I learn?

What do I do for a job?

How do we change this situation?

How do I help my mom and not have her look like she's so stressed out that she's crying?

How do we increase our financial IQ?

How do I change the path?

All of these questions were raised in my head. And then the biggest question, "Why not me?" I knew that I could and would be the person to make all these changes for myself and for my family.

The Chip on my Shoulder

I became a machine. I was willing to do whatever it took to get to an entirely new level. Everything that happened up to this point in my life contributed to the chip on my shoulder. By this time, it wasn't just about me anymore. I was hyper focused on creating generational change. I wanted to show people from my area what was actually possible. I wanted to be the person that they could look up to. I wasn't going to stop until the entire landscape was different.

At 15 years old these thoughts woke my ass up. No one was going to come do it for me. No one fucking cares. It's just the fucking truth. No one cares that you're a fourth generation coal miner. No one cares that your mom can barely pay the rent. No one cares that your dad left at 11 years old and isn't spending time with you. No one is going to come save you.

It's all on me. Once I realized that, I shouldered the 300-pound gorilla and carried him as far as I needed to produce the changes I desired. It didn't stop when I started to see the results either. The rage inside was the jet fuel that kept me going.

It was a relentlessness combined with something I loved to do. It takes all of the pieces of the puzzle to make the change. All of it. The questions you need to ask yourself are:

Are you willing to dig deep to make it happen?

Are you willing to be honest with yourself?

Are you willing to put in the work?

That's what you have to ask yourself. Being willing to do those things is the difference maker you've been looking for.

Where the Confidence Came From

At the base level, my confidence came through lifting weights. This is important to understand because the situation we were in growing up was tough. *I felt less than.* No one was telling me

I *couldn't* do something, but no one was building me up either. To be honest, no one around me was even aware.

There were never talks about doing whatever you wanted to do. There were never any discussions about finances. *It was all about survival.* If you're in an environment such as this, it's imperative to understand that there are many opportunities beyond the life you're living. You won't go anywhere in life until you start to understand this key component.

Being able to witness a few people going from coal miner to entrepreneur, and being successful with it, was very important for me. It doesn't have to be some crazy story; it just has to be impactful and meaningful to you. Embracing adversity and tackling it head on is essential to succeeding.

Fuel For the Fire

Having strong reminders to use as fuel is a powerful thing. This is especially important for the days you don't feel like doing anything. I think about my mom heating our breakfast before school with our oven because we didn't have the oil in the heater for the heat. The electric was still on, and the oven doors were open. That's how we were getting our heat.

I think about how upset she was when we didn't get the house we were supposed to get. I think about when we got evicted because we couldn't pay the rent. I think about my uncle coming over to put up a brace because the trailer was falling in. I think about motherfuckers laughing at my car when I was at the gas station because only one of my door handles worked. I had to climb through the back passenger seat. I think about my parents fighting and my dad leaving on Christmas Eve. I was only 11 years old.

I think about my dad being on strike at work and trying different businesses that never worked. I think about my grandparents and my aunt showing up in the middle of the night with groceries because my mom couldn't afford them. I think about watching my mom grind every single day waiting tables, cleaning, and making ends meet. I think about how meticulous our yard was around the trailer because my mom knew we had the shittiest house on the street. I think about the pride she maintained despite our situation.

All of that is my fuel. It lights my fire and you better fucking believe it gets me out of bed every day with a desire to win and get better.

I Wouldn't Change Anything

Was I tired of all of these things? Yes.

Was I tired of living like this? Did I hate it at the time? Yes.

Yet, at the end of the day, I wouldn't change a single thing. I tell my mom this all the time still to this day, and I would tell my dad the same if he were still alive.

If I had a different childhood and upbringing, I would have never impacted the number of people that I have. I wouldn't be me. I'm me *because* of those situations. I'm me *because* I had to fight through the adversity. I'm me *because* I had to take them head on and say, "I want something different."

I believe everyone has their own version of this. It doesn't matter if your situation isn't as severe as mine was. What's important is taking what you have, adding it to the pot, and using it as fuel to propel you forward.

The All-in Mentality

I was told that I could work as much as I wanted when I started my coal mining gig. That right there gave me a path. I could see my way out. Not only that, I was able to experience one of the most dangerous and difficult jobs on the planet - a job that three generations of my family have experienced. Once I did this job, I knew for a fact that everything else would be easy in comparison. It gave me a perspective I'll never forget.

From my coal mining experience I was able to develop modern day principles to share with the world. I knew this was about to set my life on fire. Was it easy? Absolutely not, but I was all in. Doing something hard, gaining experience, and applying what I learned was priceless. It was all I needed.

Dig Deep On Your Why

This book is about *how to* build confidence. I didn't start out as a confident person. I built confidence through lifting weights, through consistency, and through rage and hate for my situation. And because I hated it to the deepest point of my being,

I changed it forever. I constructed a plan, adjusted things when I needed to, and consistently executed at a high level.

I don't do anything special. I just don't fucking miss.

Dig deep on why you want to change your situation. Everybody wants something different. Everybody has a dream, but most give up. They give in because they don't want to dig deep to find the answers. They give in because they really don't believe it or believe in themselves.

It's easy to feel alone. There wasn't anyone around me that did what I did. There wasn't anyone around that could give me advice. No one around me understood what I was trying to do. My parents and everybody believed in me, but they didn't understand what was possible.

Well, guess what? It's all possible. I've proved it and I'm going to continue proving it.

And, it can be possible for you, too.

CHAPTER THREE

HOW I BUILT CONFIDENCE

H OW DO YOU build mental confidence? What does *mental confidence* mean to you? Do you think it's an essential factor to living a rich and fulfilling life? Do you think about it this way? Many people think about building a healthier body or the progression of their career, but never stop to consider *how to build mental confidence.*

Think about the 10,000 Rule, a concept popularized in Malcom Gladwell's book, *Outliers.* The concept says that 10,000 hours of work and dedication can make you an expert in any category, but it's a classification few ever attain. For those that do, *confidence is the result.*

How do you progress faster? Is it possible to speed up the process of building and retaining confidence? *How can you better spend your time in order to build mental confidence?*

From an Early Age

To understand the need for confidence and the impact it can have from an early age is critical for personal development. The road to becoming a more confident person has revealed two methods that have proved to be most effective.

Finding relevant information and becoming an unending student of the game.

I don't have a traditional school background. I didn't go to college to receive a two or four-year degree. I barely have a year in the system but I do have an Exercise Specialist Certificate to show for it. I have to say Columbus State Community College was perfect for me. Everyone's path with education is different, but I've learned over time that in life, we're actually always learning.

I used to think reading was stupid. As I write my second book, I'm completely baffled that this was once a part of my thought process. I've always had a negative opinion towards traditional schooling because of my experience growing up. I felt like I was being forced to learn subjects I had zero interest in, making the taste in my mouth even worse. All I was interested in was doubling down and going 20 levels deeper on the topics that interested me.

Over time, I learned the value of reading and learning from others to deepen that knowledge bank. I realized that I didn't have to stick to what school was teaching, and I've kept that desire for personal development and knowledge discovery going throughout my whole life.

Building My Education

The year was 1999. I was in dire need of a real-world education. The internet wasn't yet the wealth of knowledge we know today, and the only resources at my disposal consisted of conversations with people, books, and cassette tapes. That's it.

What books did I need to read? What tapes did I need to listen to? How could I ultimately improve myself? These were some of the questions I asked myself as I ventured down the rabbit hole. My education base grew, and my love for learning and absorbing pertinent information took off at a rapid pace.

It doesn't matter whether it's about dieting, business, or a process. Proper education in your field is the catalyst to making you both more comfortable and confident, especially when it comes time for application. As soon as I took this seriously every day, I instantly started to become more confident. I believe a lot of people stop learning once they leave school, but I actually did the opposite. I started taking it more seriously once I left. I realized again that the burden of success was all on me. It was only me that could help me, so I needed to develop myself at an entirely different level.

Get Uncomfortable

Don't get it twisted: exposure to uncomfortable situations is where true growth lies. You don't change while you're in your comfort zone. For example, I purposely get up early to start the process of learning *before* the day's distractions compete for my attention. Explicitly and consistently allocating time for reading and study ensures that I'm able to put in the work.

I wish I could tell you that I had a lights-out, foolproof strategy at age 20, but I can't. At this point, I had read a few impactful books and went to a few seminars. Momentum was beginning to build, but my consistency needed work. In reality, I was still a kid with no guidance trying to figure it out.

That's why I'm writing this book. If I had seen something like this when I was 20 years old, it would have been a game changer for me. I want this book to be that for you, and I know we can help you achieve the goals you want to accomplish.

Studying icons such as Arnold, Andrew Carnegie, and Napoleon Hill along with practical application of that knowledge deepened my understanding for a multitude of different scenarios.

Situations and lessons I read about supplied me with a general blueprint for navigating through life and becoming successful. Hours of application and education will undeniably strengthen your decision-making skills, ultimately molding you into a more confident individual. More confidence in everyday life allows you to take more risks in order to win. Cultivating a mindset of resilience allows you to win. *Expect to win. Never to lose.*

This process took me over 20 years. The resources of the early 2000's weren't nearly at the level they are today. No one told me how to do this or handed me the keys to the castle. The good news? You can go faster! Modern technology has allowed information and knowledge to be readily available with the click of a button. Take advantage! I would have loved the stuff available nowadays. Shit, I still can't believe the resources.

Be Intentional

What line of work are you truly passionate about? What drives you to get up out of bed every morning?

For me, it was the world of fitness and helping people. The funny thing is I didn't know a single fitness professional growing up. It was like a fake job that didn't exist!

Honestly, in 1997-98 when I really started thinking that going into the fitness business was my ultimate move, people thought I was crazy. I told the coal miners on my first day underground

I wanted to be a personal trainer. To them, that was crazy because the only image that came to mind for them when they heard the term "personal trainer" was Richard Simmons.

If you're under 40, you'll probably need to Google him, and you'll probably laugh when you do. But, seriously, that's what people thought of as success back then in personal training. That wasn't what I wanted, but the people around me, especially in the coal mines, didn't get it.

People didn't understand how I could make a living as a trainer and lifting weights. They saw that as a hobby, and now it is my job. I remind people often that lifting weights isn't just a hobby for me; it's a fucking job - one that I love.

What do I need to know in order to be more mentally confident?

Objectively answering this question immediately propelled me in the right direction. I made better decisions with my clients, training programs, and in my business. Slicing up the pie allowed me to focus on each component to make my business stronger.

What did I do? I created a strategy and system that would produce higher mental confidence. I started with studying the best of the best. Who is the best in the bodybuilding world? Arnold Schwarzenegger.

Everything Arnold

I read and watched everything I could get my hands on that was based around Arnold Schwarzenegger. Eventually, I was fortunate enough to learn from him personally, but this didn't occur until the *15-year mark* on my journey of self-confidence. I logged countless hours and years on my own confidence journey before I even met Arnold.

Learning and understanding Arnold's principles, mentality, and thought process changed my life forever. I never came away from working alongside Arnold thinking I could accomplish less, that's for sure. I walked out of those meetings knowing what I was capable of and ready to conquer the world.

I would say Arnold understands what's possible maybe more than anyone I have ever been around because he literally built the life he wanted through hard work, perseverance, and belief. I came away each time more inspired and asking myself why I didn't push more and dream bigger. He made me realize that it's all possible.

You're currently reading one of those dreams. Me as an author? I dreamed about it. Now, I've made it happen.

Like I always say, I don't just *kinda* want it. I *absolutely* fucking want it. I want it all!

What About Strength?

Having the ability to build and construct an effective strength program for my clients and I was crucial. I needed to learn more about powerlifting and the principles behind strength training. I started by printing off every article that Louie Simmons and Westside Barbell published, placing and organizing them into a binder. It didn't stop there. I actively sought out people from Westside Barbell to learn even more.

If you don't know about Westside, it's one of the strongest gyms in the world. The training methods from Westside have changed the game entirely in the world of powerlifting and athletic training, and I learned so much from them over the years.

I came across John Broz, of Average Broz Gym in Las Vegas, who's responsible for bringing the Bulgarian and Squat Every

Day methodology to America. I flew to Vegas to learn and train with him, eventually becoming friends still to this day.

As you can see, my goal was to broaden my knowledge and learn from experts in the field. This is a tried and true method to getting better. By getting better and understanding more, you'll naturally build confidence.

Total Immersion

Dive deep, even if you're not the best. Understanding a subject in its entirety produces the confidence you seek.

I totally immersed myself into the bodybuilding world, competing in 15 shows. I read all of the muscle magazines, contributed to publications, and connected with people in the industry. Then, when the opportunity to meet Arnold Schwarzenegger arose, the 15 years of practical experience and study carried me through with flying colors. I knew the content to such a level that you would have thought I lived in the 1970's alongside him. He could see and feel it during the meeting.

I learned everything I could from the Westside Barbell legends and their powerlifting philosophies. I wanted to understand what it felt like to squat 700 pounds and to be coached by some of the best strength coaches that ever lived. I was even willing to go to the extreme degree of weighing a lifetime-high 240 pounds. This was not a quality 240 pounds let me tell you. I'm not made to weigh that much.

I was completely all in with cellulite on my legs - the whole nine yards!

I wanted to learn and understand why the Bulgarians squatted every day. My squat every day quest began, squatting every day for *three years straight*. Over those three years I hit every one of my lifting goals and produced some of the most unique content that has ever hit Bodybuilding.com, racking in over 50 million-page views. *My career changed forever.*

Total immersion, commitment, and dedication to a subject will eventually elevate you to expert status. For me, it was my craft as a personal trainer. As a bodybuilder. As a powerlifter. As an athlete.

I was studying and absorbing as much information as possible, for every style of diet out there. I tried keto, intermittent fasting, traditional bodybuilding, carb rotation/cycling, Atkins and the Anabolic Diet. Anything I heard or read about, I tried. I truly was the guinea pig. Years of trial & error allowed me to help thousands of people with my signature *Anabolic Fasting protocol.*

Due to full immersion with these topics, I became both more comfortable and more confident. Consistent experimentation and education allowed me to ascend to the expert level. *My mental and physical confidence soared.*

As I write this book, I'm zooming in on subjects such as tendon health, jumping, and overall explosiveness. The results thus far have been staggering, especially as a now 43-year-old athlete.

I will always lead by example. I'm teaching and displaying simultaneously. I've become a resource for those that need help. You can become a resource by practicing what you preach. Improve your understanding by seeking out new information and resources with alternative viewpoints. Doing this makes your game stronger. It's a lifelong cycle and pursuit of learning, applying and testing.

Study it. Apply it. Live it. That's how you achieve true mental confidence within your craft.

Self-Education & the Business World

When I was about 20 years old, I read a book called *Conversations with Millionaires*, with Robert Kiyosaki as one of the authors. The book was given to me by my friend Mark Evans, DM. This book opened my eyes to the basic fundamentals of business that I was previously unaware of.

For example, I didn't even know the difference between a *liability and an asset.* Without a basic comprehension of these concepts, it's near impossible to understand how debt works, overhead costs, margins, cash flow, or how to read a profit and loss statement. They don't teach these concepts in the classroom.

Intentionally allocating time to self-education filled the lack of schooling gap. Then, when it came time to sign a lease for my first gym at 20 years old, I could actually understand what was going on.

Education and research helped me to structure deals. I learned how to assemble investors in order to buy equipment for my gym, as well as how to return their investment. I learned quickly how taxes work for an entrepreneur. Without taxes being automatically withheld, I was forced to learn how and when to pay Uncle Sam. I learned the ins and outs of effectively marketing a small business with little to no budget. I learned the harsh realities of how fast I could lose everything by signing a lease for three years with no money in the bank.

I had nothing to lose because there was nothing to gain.

What does the risk/reward look like? What does the budget look like? How do I handle my bookkeeping? How do I market my business? How do I set my pay scale, raise my rates or cut deals with clients? *How do I make it?*

These are the questions that you need to be asking yourself as you figure out your career and life. Addressing these questions now and coming up with a plan will prevent future struggles.

You Are in Charge

Constantly learn and try new things to see what works best. Many people see my position today and think that much of what I earned came naturally. It didn't.

I read every piece of content put out by Robert Kiyosaki, Andrew Carnegie and Napoleon Hill. I have an extensive library on my phone, as well as at my house. If you told me when I was younger that's what would happen as I got older, I would have thought you were crazy.

When I was younger, I thought reading was dumb. Going to college after high school wasn't on my radar. I thought learning was something reserved only for the rich. I thought reading wasn't something that would matter to me or be helpful to me. I thought that us country guys would only work blue-collar type jobs.

Then, I started to realize that I'm fully in control of everything, and that included my personal education. Self-education costs quite a bit less than the thousands of dollars that private institutions charge! Even if you go to school at any level, you and you alone are ultimately responsible for your education.

Trial & Error

Should I have this many people per hour? Should I have them pay monthly or weekly? Can I put one person in a group session? Could I put five people in and still charge the same amount? Should I add a gym fee as my business grows? Should I have trainers rent space?

These are some of the questions I was asking myself and challenges I was facing when first starting my business. I had to experiment and see what would work and see what wouldn't work.

I believe that I'm now at the top end of the personal training industry. I attribute much of that success to the 20+ years of education, trials, and errors I made along the way.

Success in training. Success in business. Success in life.

Success relies on your ability to make educated, confident decisions over and over again. That's all.

Take the person who has repeatedly made bad decisions throughout their lives. Bad decisions, compounded over time, lead to destruction. Will you make bad decisions along the way? Of course, making bad decisions along the way is an inescapable inevitability. However, bad decisions may have a silver lining. They have the capability to teach confidence. If I'm experimenting with a lifting protocol and it doesn't work out, I'm able to alter my strategy to make the appropriate fix. A bad decision eliminates a possibility, ultimately bringing you closer to the solution.

I feel the same way in the business arena. If I create or do something that doesn't work, then I can shift my focus to finding the solution that does work. I'm confident that I can figure it out.

This confidence is cultivated through years of studying and dedication to the craft. I understand the background and calculate the risk when making my decisions. I have the expectation to win.

Some read this as arrogance or that I have my head in the sand or that I only think positive. It's not like that at all. It's due to the hours and years I've spent molding myself into a more confident being.

If I'm risking my money and time into a project, I expect it to work. And if it doesn't work out 100%, I will alter my approach in order to find the winning strategy.

Do you feel the confidence radiating through these pages? The confidence flowing through these pages is due to the time involved and dedication to the craft as a fitness entrepreneur.

It starts by fully understanding fitness, lifting, strength, explosiveness, and programming at an expert level. The second half of the equation involves being able to effectively run the business. Executed successfully, this means I'm creating quality products and building robust business systems that I know how to scale. It means marketing the product in a smart manner and having a clear future vision for the business.

It can be a lot to handle. This is not an easy deal. That's why being successful is so fucking hard.

But, I can guarantee you that it's all worth it in the end.

Studying & Time Involved

The hours dedicated to studying, applying and experimenting are mandatory. Personally, I knew the traditional college education route wasn't for me, aside from one year at Columbus State Community College.

No one was going to hold my hand. The majority of people I was learning and studying from are people I would never meet. No one was there to save me. *It was all on me.*

At the same time, realizing it was all on me was freeing. I knew it was up to me, and that meant I needed to make a plan and execute.

What I Knew

I know how bad I want it. My aim back then and still to this day is to change future family generations for the better. The countless hours and minutes devoted to my studies and trials have been worth the effort. Consistently expanding and challenging my boundaries and limits is what it takes. I knew that I had to be extreme, or even obsessive.

I've been fortunate enough to have made many great decisions throughout my career. It's crucial to understand that these decisions were not a result of *pure luck*. Do you get lucky sometimes? Take it from Gary Player: "The more I practice, the luckier I get."

Mental confidence is essential when it comes to making better decisions. Over the last several years, the development of my mental confidence has permitted me to make clear, concise, and composed decisions. These decisions have compounded over time into results that I'm proud of. I'm not pumping my chest but rather I'm trying to over communicate just how difficult it is to get to the top.

Bet on Yourself

The only person that is going to help you is you. You must cultivate a non-negotiable mentality in order to continually improve yourself. Don't go 50 percent; go the full 100 percent. Many miss the mark here, and many say they are giving 100 percent but aren't being honest with themselves. Many trainers may do a great job with learning their craft, but then completely miss the second half of the picture: *the business side.* You must put the same amount of stock into both variables.

I'm not a D-1 caliber athlete with loads of natural talent, but I can tell you with full confidence that I've squeezed every ounce of possibility out of this body. Everything. I live to challenge, test and demand more from my body, even as a 43-year-old athlete. *I don't just kind of want it.*

The same concept applies directly to my business. I'm regularly pushing myself to create new relationships, learn new or more efficient ways of doing business, and learning how to better manage risk to be more successful.

Is my time over? Absolutely not. What you're currently reading is part of the process. I'm striving to educate future family members that I will never meet.

To My Kids
Alex, Madelyn, and Anden,

When you read this - whether or not I'm around - I want you to understand that I wanted your life to be different. I wanted to teach you what it takes to love what you do and be successful.

Read or listen to my voice knowing how serious I was about making impactful change in our lives. I did it for you, and now I'm able to teach that same process to many more.

As I record and write this book in 2021, I'm thinking about someone in 2060 reading this. The content within these pages is *timeless. It will never change.*

20 Years

It's taken 20 years to exude this level of confidence and conviction. I believe the words I'm saying wholeheartedly. One million fucking percent. Why not 100 percent? Because that's how aggressive you have to be. Going one million percent incites feeling and emotion. It gives you an edge.

There's no halfway-in when it comes to being an expert. It must be real, authentic, and aggressive. You have to be willing to do what others aren't willing to do.

I didn't get up at 3:00am today, I got up at 2:30am. I didn't do it because I needed more money. I got up this early because I wanted to take this project more seriously. I wanted to take my jumping goal more seriously. I wanted to take my life more seriously. Armed with perseverance and a non-negotiable attitude, I'm able to clarify my thoughts to take my mental confidence to the next level.

What About You?

I'm here to check your mental confidence. Are you doing the right things in life to improve yourself? Are you doing those things that are going to give you mental clarity and confidence? That's my challenge to you. Take stock of your life and what you're currently doing. Be honest with yourself, and make changes if you need to.

Throughout this book I will show you the structures and systems you need in order to build stronger mental confidence and the mentality it takes to win at a non-negotiable level.

You have to hear it. You have to read it. You have to understand it. Think about the compounded power of the pages and audio you read and listen to over one, three, 10, or 20 years. How's your confidence look then? What will your decisions look like?

Only then will you grasp the true essence of confidence.

CHAPTER FOUR

HOW DOES CONFIDENCE RUN YOUR LIFE?

YOU MAY HAVE never thought about how much of an impact confidence can have on your life, but I would argue that it's one of the most important tools to develop each and every day.

My entire morning strategy is built around drills to build confidence. *Confidence* isn't something that you accomplish and be done with. It's an ongoing quest that constantly needs work and reinforcement in order to be able to handle anything thrown your way.

Waking up

You wake up. You look in the mirror. You decide what you're going to wear for the day. What you decide projects how confident you are.

How do I look in this shirt? How do these pants fit? Does my butt look big? Do I look or feel bloated? What will people think of me? Am I comfortable in my skin? Am I feeling confident?

Listen, I used to weigh 240 pounds at one point in my life. The shirt would go on, but my stomach would be slightly showing, my chest wouldn't feel tight, and my sides would be sticking out. Talk about not feeling confident and being self conscious.

For the majority of people, *confidence starts with the body*. That in turn directly affects *the mind*. How could it not? Physical fitness and confidence go hand in hand, and I'm living proof of that.

Feeling great, being lean and energetic, and having your clothes fit properly will give you a better chance to walk out of the house as a confident individual. It's a whole new ball game when you can believe in yourself. The reflection in the mirror of a healthy and fit body and the confidence to follow through breed a positive mentality.

Seek the Spotlight

I've always been a big believer in forcing yourself into being comfortable with the uncomfortable. Maybe you have an upcoming presentation at work. Maybe you have a big date coming up. Maybe you have a big game on the horizon. Whatever the case, where many crumble, *the spotlight,* you can thrive.

Confidence will be your close companion when you take center stage. They say that more people have the fear of public speaking than dying. Little do they know that this fear is usually due to a lack of confidence, and even fewer people realize that confidence can be developed and earned.

I actively seek opportunities in the spotlight. I want the ball. Even though I may not knock it out of the park every time, it's important to seize these moments. Regular exposure will better prepare you for future opportunities, and reps in the spotlight will make you want to seek it out even more. It all compounds on itself.

You walked out of the house feeling and looking good for a reason. You don't just magically wake up feeling good and confident, especially as you get older. Properly exercising your mind and body supplies you with the confidence to take on anything that comes your way. Even though you won't feel 10 out of 10 every day, it's key to give yourself a chance to fucking win and to also have something to fall back on when times are tough. It's important because good decisions are made based on confidence in yourself.

The Arnold Pitch

I know because I've experienced both sides of the coin - to feel on top of the world and to be at the bottom. I know what it feels like to be overweight, and I know what it feels like to weigh 180-185 pounds and be abso-fucking-lutely shredded. I know what it feels like to be on a magazine cover with my three children and to have that same magazine thrown to my idol, Arnold Schwarzenegger, during a business pitch. I wasn't even the one who brought the magazine! Talk about a game changer.

Arnold looks at the magazine and goes, "This is you? Your abs remind me of Frank Zane's a little bit." Holy shit. To hear these words come out of his mouth threw me into a state of disbelief. To be on a cover with my kids, while also sitting in Arnold's office pitching him, was a surreal experience.

I vividly remember sitting in that chair. I was ready for this moment because I had worked my whole life for a shot like this. I was fully confident in my abilities to answer and explain *any* question that Arnold posed to me. My goal was to let him know that I wasn't leaving that office without being his business partner.

What I want you to takeaway from this experience is that I didn't just show up to that meeting and get the deal out of luck. I worked my ASS off, and that gave me the confidence to be prepared for the meeting and to impress Arnold enough to do business with me. That confidence came from my daily choices and daily sacrifices. That's what you can implement in your own life, and you'll be amazed at the success.

The consistent discipline I had instilled throughout my life came to the forefront simultaneously. Everything aligned for this moment. The result was *respect*. Respect from the man I have been deeply inspired by for my entire life.

Confidence runs the world.

Opportunity

If I hadn't pushed that hard through the diet phase, hadn't gotten that cover done, and that investor hadn't thrown the magazine to him in our meeting, it could have turned out completely different. *My life* could have turned out completely different.

Opportunity called my name. I would have never been ready for a moment like this if I hadn't been working on my confidence. Fully preparing and knowing the material like it was the back of my hand allowed me to speak with conviction. I wasn't worried because I knew I had the answers. I never even considered a negative outcome from the meeting because I was so confident in getting what I wanted.

Not only was I working on my physical confidence, but my mental game as well. These facets aligned at the exact moment I needed them for this meeting with Arnold. All the hours, all the sweat, and all the dreams. This was my moment to change my life forever.

Everything You Do

Every opportunity and every decision you make comes down to *confidence.* The confidence in your decision-making. The confidence with how you feel and the confidence in your own mentality. Confidence can help you persevere through any set of circumstances despite what anyone else says.

I have confidence in my abilities. I have confidence in my being. I have confidence in knowing what I want for myself. *All of it.* To progress forward is impossible without it.

I wasn't born this way. That's not how it works. You have to be willing to put in the work. Do you have a strategy in place *right now to change your mentality?*

That's where I come in. I can help lead you down a path to be a more confident person. Everything changes when your confidence increases. It's some next-level type shit, and I want you to experience it in the same way that I have.

My goal is to write a legendary book on how to build confidence because it is the ultimate difference-maker in life. The biggest thing people get wrong with confidence is thinking that it comes from external sources. It comes from within. It comes from the daily decisions we make. It comes from showing the fuck up and putting in the work.

It Runs the World

Confidence runs your world whether you like it or not. You can either take ownership of your own mentality around confidence or let it take control of you.

Are you aimlessly wandering through life each day? Are you asking yourself if this is really what you want out of your life and your career?

Maybe you're thinking to yourself that things aren't going the way you want them to. Maybe you aren't regularly working on yourself, or maybe you don't have a strategy in place. Or, maybe, you just think that you're too busy for it all.

This type of person will have difficulty making decisions and pushing through obstacles. They will always struggle, and they will always feel tired and behind. Conversely, confidence strengthens your decision-making abilities. It fuels your energy. I would argue that a higher percentage of confident decisions are made right, rather than wrong. I have proven this to be true time and time again.

Make your decisions based on the experiences you've had in your field, work, craft, mental training, and physical training. Make decisions based on gut intuition and time involved. And, learn from those decisions. Doing so will produce successful results.

Success is nothing but your ability *to respond* to a set of decisions over and over and over again.

Positive always outweighs negative. Optimism outlasts pessimism. Confident people are more positive people; they're more optimistic people, too. This doesn't mean that you have your head in the sand, only ever looking at the positives and not addressing the negatives. Rather, it means having a glass half-full outlook on the world and understanding that there is something positive to be taken out of every situation.

There's always a solution.

There's always a way.

There's always more to learn.

There's always more to work on.

There's always a strategy to get better.

Reading these pages marks the beginning of your journey. Implement the plan that we'll discuss to yield the long-term results you crave. Join the Cory G community to meet like minded people like yourself and learn from them. Go into this battle together with me and with them. Then when you're up against a difficult, important decision, you will *know* what's best for you. You will be able to *feel* what's best for you.

It'll be your motherfucking gameday. You've been preparing for this. Put me in coach, I'm fucking ready.

The Gamer Mentality

The gamer mentality - not many have it.

Why do the GOATs of all sports, like Michael Jordan, Tiger Woods, and other legends, seem to always have this mentality? CONFIDENCE.

I've never been around MJ, but I've been fortunate to have spent some time with Tiger Woods.

Why is Tiger so great? Because of his preparation and mentality. That man has hit *millions* of golf balls. When he approaches a shot to win a tournament, he *believes* he can walk on water with that golf club. He's also hit the exact shot he needs to hit under pressure in practice a thousand times. Just like when I'm going to squat or deadlift in a meet - I've repped that bitch out a million times before and I KNOW I'm going get that lift.

Tiger is an entirely different breed of competitor. He has prepared himself for battle in order to make the highest-level shots in the sport. He *believes* that he can be the greatest of all time. When I interviewed him, I asked him, "What do you get up every day to do?" Before I could even finish my sentence, he replied, "To win."

If that doesn't fire you the fuck up, I don't know what will.

A Small Piece

Michael Jordan, Tiger Woods, David Goggins, and others like this are in the extreme category. What if we could even take a small piece from their playbook? A piece that we can inject into our lives. What if I showed you a proven path to incrementally raise your confidence? Compounded over time, this path will help you construct a more confident version of yourself.

Here's the catch: you have to be the Michael Jordan, Tiger Woods, and David Goggins of your life. No one else can do it for you. Start following these strategies and techniques *now* in order to put yourself on the fast-track.

What it Feels Like

It's an incredible feeling to know what you want *with certainty*. To know what you want and believe you can do it. And to know that it's backed up by hard work.

These are proven principles that have been repeated time after time throughout history. I'm here to decipher and explain the patterns that will take your confidence game to a new level. I don't think it will, I know it will. Why do I know it will work? I know it because I live it every day, and I've used these same principles to take my life from a trailer to owning multiple successful businesses and having financial freedom.

I may not be MJ or Tiger Woods, but I've built my personal confidence through sweat, work, belief and perseverance. That is how I got here, not because I was born into a rich family or because I got lucky.

It's because I don't just *kind of* want it. I knew that the determining factor to my long-term success would be my ability to confidently make decisions consistently over time.

That's what I built. That's what I continue to build. And that's what I'm going to help you build.

CHAPTER FIVE

NON-NEGOTIABLE
HABITS

'M GOING TO turn the clock all the way back to eighth grade. I'm at the beginning of my career with lifting weights, and I'm starting to see some little baby muscles pop out. Between lifting weights and organized sports, the foundation of my personal confidence is beginning to take shape.

I practiced relentlessly. I never missed team practices, I never missed personal practice sessions, and I never missed a lifting session. I became a disciple of Arnold Schwarzenegger. I read everything I could get my hands on. Arnold preached the value of consistency and the importance of building these blocks every day. It helped form my sense of identity, and those learnings from Arnold still continue to shape me today.

No Matter What

Then, when I began having results, many people took notice and wanted to come lift with me. I thought to myself, "Yeah, of course I'd love to have a training partner." I thought if I could have a training partner like Franco, Ed Corney and the guys I read about, that would be great. I thought that if that's how Arnold does it, that's how I need to do it.

Throughout eighth grade, I would get guys coming through for two or three weeks at a time. They wouldn't see immediate results and quit after a few weeks. It wasn't until my sophomore year in high school that I had a *consistent* training partner.

We all wanted to get better. At that time, I was beginning to see progress because I was willing to put in the time and work required. I was willing *to show up no matter what.* I wasn't familiar with the term "non-negotiable" at the time, but I began to understand the true value of simply showing up every day. I could see the results that I wanted. All I had to was show up.

I didn't know how long it would take to look this way. I didn't know how long it would take to get that strong. All I knew was that I was making *incremental improvements* every day and that I would get there if I stuck with it. If I knew what I was doing was working, why would I change anything? Why would I stop this steam engine that's gaining momentum?

Lock in

When a non-negotiable habit is giving you a positive result, lock onto it. So, what happened sophomore year? I ran into Dustin Myers. Dustin is someone who felt the same way I did about not missing workouts, staying locked in, and pushing each other. The momentum continued to build all the way through senior year.

Dustin and I still share this bond today as brothers, workout partners, and business partners. That same daily drive and not missing drive us both to this day.

Missing is Unacceptable

I'm now 43 years old. To this day, missing workouts for any period of time is simply unacceptable. I've always been this way, and I always will. I realized that if I showed up, even when I didn't want to, even when there were a bunch of excuses, even when things weren't going great, that I would still positively benefit in some way. *No matter what.*

Committing to this habit is one of the smartest things that I've ever done in my entire life. Sure, there are things that weight-lifting can't fix or make you feel better. In my personal experience over the past 20+ years, I've always felt and performed better when I stayed dedicated to the process. Through injuries, through hardships, through all of it.

Being dedicated to something, especially a fitness related goal like weightlifting, has the unique ability to translate into other parts of your life.

Non-negotiable Habits Apply Everywhere

I took what I learned in the gym and applied the same principles across every category in my life. That's it. That's my not so secret secret. I tackled my businesses just like I approached a heavy squat in the gym. I approached my personal development just like a heavy deadlift. I went all in, all the time.

Not all disciplines are created equal; I get that. But, when you can wrap your non-negotiable habits around what you want to accomplish, then you become an immovable force. It's the ultimate difference-maker.

I started my first personal training business in 1999 when I was only 20 years old. In the early days I couldn't train until 7 a.m. because I had clients at 5 a.m. I never missed a 7 a.m. training session because I was already there at the gym. As my business grew, things changed and I had to start getting up earlier to train before my clients. My training time changed from 7 a.m. to 5 a.m.

When Everything Changed

People automatically assume that they can't train early in the morning. They'll use every excuse in the book to get out of it. Well, here's where everything changed. About 10 years ago, we made the switch to start training at 4 a.m. While it's true that everyone has their own unique schedule, there's no excuse to *not* train at 4 a.m.

The switch to 4 a.m. not only changed me, it changed the entire group. To train at 4 a.m. became legendary. Why? Because at 4 a.m. there are no excuses to not be there except for being lazy.

No matter what you do in your professional life, you can be free at 4am. Our crew now has all types of people ranging from a professor to blue collar workers. You can still make it to work, there's no one calling you, and there usually aren't any family obligations to attend to. The only thing present is your *supreme discipline*. Your supreme discipline is the only thing available to you at that time.

Why 4am?

People always say, "I don't know how you do it." It all began with the streak of momentum at 5 a.m. Then, when I went to another level at 4 a.m., it became a non-negotiable habit.

No matter what, I'm there.

I show up at 4 a.m. because I know what types of results it yields. You may be reading this thinking, "Cory, you're a fitness guy. It's easy for you to do it at 4 a.m."

Guess what? No, it's not.

It wouldn't matter. I work out with a group over 20 and have thousands of members on CoryG Fitness that have subscribed to this mentality.

It's this very mentality that has produced extreme focus in my life. Training at 4 a.m. took my physique, strength, and focus to the next level. It's a total separator that puts me out front and helps me set the tone for every day.

Can you get the same results if you train at another time? Sure, but here's the question. When else in your day are you going to experience complete, uninterrupted time? *It's almost impossible for most people because the world is loud and full of distractions.*

Take this book for example. What time did I get up to write? *Before* my 4 a.m. workout because no one even knows that I'm awake. This is the same exact strategy I used to finish my last book. No one was there to bother me and there were no distractions. And that also means there are no excuses. It was me and my thoughts entirely. All I cared about was executing.

When It Gets Hard

Take inventory of your own life. What are the non-negotiable things that you've had trouble sticking to in the past when things have gotten difficult? Don't feel bad about it; it's common, and it's happened to every single one of us at some point.

Walking lunges are a great example of this. Lunges are difficult, but I knew that if I could put together a streak it would take both my mind and body to the next level. The streak I created consisted of lunging 800 meters every day. My morning routine was to lift weights, then lunge half a mile. Once I took the lunges seriously, my training took off exponentially.

Building a 300-day streak was far from easy. It didn't matter how sore I was. It didn't matter whether I had a powerlifting meet or a bodybuilding show. It didn't matter if I had a photoshoot or if I was traveling. Do you understand what I'm saying? I made time every day, and I didn't fucking miss.

The dedication to the streak produced insane results. My legs were jacked, my strength numbers were through the roof, and I had the fastest metabolism of my entire career. I was looking jacked and peeled at the same time while putting up some insane numbers in the gym.

Develop Your Strategy

What is your non-negotiable strategy? What systems do you have in place to be great? Are you working towards that? How do I get to where I want to be, and what do I have to do every single day, no matter what, to get there?

These are the questions you need to be asking yourself at this point in the book. You can copy my systems and use weightlifting as your center to build around. Or, you can create your own system that works for you.

You're not going to have all the answers right away - and that's okay. The important thing is to get started. Ask yourself these questions, and then answer them *honestly*. I can only display what has worked for me personally. I'm talking about the early morning workout, the walking lunges, and the personal development material.

Strategically implementing these non-negotiable habits first thing in the morning gives me my clearest mind to think. I've checked the boxes on all these hard things before my "day" has even started.

Focus on What's Possible

If I hit my non-negotiable habits early, how could I *not* be prepared for whatever's thrown my way during the day? This statement has rung true to me for over 10 years and counting.

Getting up at 3 a.m. to train at 4 a.m. and lifting heavy is hard. Lunging afterwards no matter the weather is hard. And, that's why I love it. Once I make it through those non-negotiables in the morning, I know I can tackle anything that comes my way that day because it won't be as hard as what I just did.

I'm getting my lifting and conditioning out of the way. I'm listening to audiobooks or podcasts on the way to the gym, and on the way home. I'm getting a chance to structure my day before anyone wakes up. When done consistently over time, the results are often mind-blowing. I saw the outcome and became addicted to how good it felt to execute. You want to become addicted to the process and strive to reach that level where it feels good to do these things every morning.

Ignore what time of day it is. Ignore the number of hours that society tells you need to sleep. Ignore the cousin that told you that it's not going to work. Funnel all your time and energy into what is *actually working*. Only think about what is *actually happening*. Only think about the result that is *actually possible* and what you *actually want to do.*

Once I stopped paying attention to all these distractions, my entire view expanded. It didn't matter what this or that person thought. *They're not you, they don't have the same goals, and sometimes they simply don't understand what you're trying to accomplish.*

That's okay. It's not your responsibility to make them understand. It is your responsibility, however, to know when you need to listen to yourself over the others in your life.

If you place your goals and expectations around what *someone else* thinks, then you're going to get *someone else's* goals. I don't know about you, but I don't want someone else's goals. I want mine.

Streaks & Momentum

I know what it's going to take to get to where I want to go and where you want to go. I know because of the time I've put in, the streaks I've created, and the things I've accomplished throughout my career. Have you ever done anything *100 days in a row?* Have you ever done anything 200 days in a row other than brush your teeth? Think about it.

Have you ever created your own streaks in order to build momentum to realize your goals? If you haven't, then you need to check yourself. For example, if you want to get smarter with a subject, then you need to read about it for a *half hour every day for the next year.*

If you want to get in shape, then you need to walk, lunge, whatever, every day. If you're physically capable of doing walking lunges, you should participate in *Lunge & Learn* – lunging 400-800 meters while listening to an audio book every day. You will be amazed at the results mentally and physically that discipline and streaks can create.

Maintaining a streak of 100, 200, or 300 days, will change you completely. Reflect on this for a moment. The *Lunge & Learn* template consists of lunging for time and distance while listening to an audio book. You're getting stronger, increasing your muscular endurance, and increasing your metabolism, all while getting smarter in the process.

We all love multitasking, so why not put it to good use for your mind and body?

Guess what? There's even an added bonus. I'm talking about a similar feeling to the "runner's high." It's a next-level cheat code. Once you commit to these streaks, you crave that "runner's high" feeling and it keeps you coming back.

Then, when you combine this time of self-improvement with non-negotiable dedication, you become an unstoppable force.

How could you *not* improve? You're only not improving if you choose to not improve. That's it. It may sound simple, but it's true.

The choice is yours.

- Do I want to put a streak together to improve myself?
- Do I want to get to the next level in my work, my job, my business, or me as a person?

Ask yourself these questions:

- What are a few streaks that you can put together *now* to take you to the next level?
- What kind of streaks can you put together *now* that are going to help you build confidence?

Non-negotiable habits + execution + time. It works.

Confidence is earned. Daily streaks and non-negotiables are part of earning and building that confidence. Start building your strong foundation of confidence. Doing so will better equip you for the big presentation, for the big ask, or for the next business you start.

Non-negotiable Habits

You can rely on confidence that is built through non-negotiable habits and streaks. Think about school. Now, I don't love everything that we teach in school, but I'm pretty sure it's a non-negotiable habit. They're forcing you to learn certain things consistently over time.

What do you think about when a trainer has an appointment for you every Monday, Wednesday, and Friday?

What do you think work is? They're all non-negotiable habits that we've accepted and committed to.

Force those habits in your life that you know will make you better. Force yourself to do the hard things that you know will make you better. The key is to find out what those things are. You must identify them first, and then dedicate yourself to them.

For me, I've identified what will make me different. I've identified those things that I know will separate me, then executed at the highest level. Doing so has allowed me to live the life I've always wanted. Now it's time for you to do the same.

CHAPTER SIX

IT DIDN'T WORK

I T DIDN'T WORK. It didn't work cause you're not there yet mentally. It didn't work because you needed to be more curious and take in more knowledge. It didn't work because you have to put in more work.

The foundation of confidence must be strong, not fragile. Cracks in the foundation will lead to you giving up. That's why everything we've talked about up to this point is so important. The foundation you rely on must be built strong from the beginning.

Believing it Will Work

You are working with the pursuit of the long game. No one is entitled to a particular timeline of success, and you have to fall in love with the journey and the process. That being said, *you must believe that it will work.* Whether it's your business, relationships, or building a better body, it doesn't matter - you just have to believe.

This core principle is difficult for many to grasp. When they don't see results quickly, their confidence takes a hit. They backtrack, or worse, *they give up.* Because they give up, their confidence takes a massive blow and they have to start all over from scratch.

In my situation, my goal was to lift weights and get paid to do it. It almost makes me laugh saying this out loud because the goal seems so simple now. It was so simple back then.

I remember thinking, "if I could lift weights and get paid, *then I'm winning.*" It was just a fact. My career, which also happens to be my hobby, has evolved in a major way over the past 20 plus years. It didn't start with me having my own fitness app and platform to help thousands of people. Not even close. It started as a personal trainer helping one person at a time, making $20 per hour. Don't gloss over this because I know what it feels like to feel "stuck." I know what it feels like when things aren't happening fast enough.

As human beings, we naturally seek the path of least resistance. It's much easier to stay the same, or even progress backwards, than it is to *progress forward*. It's why so many people stay in situations similar to the ones they were born into or grew up in. So, the choice is yours. Are you going to continue being upset with yourself? Are you going to just give up?

Or are you going to keep working? Are you going to seek ways to make yourself better? Are you going to put in the mandatory work to build up a higher level of confidence so you can seize the next opportunity?

How Do You Know?

When it comes to creating opportunities or opportunities presenting themselves, I'm highly optimistic. Why do I assume this? I know this because I've experienced it time and time again. I know what the process yields. Although I'm not entitled to a certain time, I know that opportunities will eventually show themselves. It's up to you to be prepared for them. It's up to you to recognize them.

Proper preparation prevents poor performance. The 5 P's. Keep that in mind throughout this journey.

I'm going to continue my process of trial and error. I'm going to continually try out different combinations of diet plans and exercises to see what works best. I'm going to immerse myself with those subjects I want to learn so I can eventually teach it to others. If my focus is constantly on pushing to make myself better, building confidence, and personal development, then I know it's just a matter of time. *These are the variables I can control.* And I know that if I keep this pattern, then opportunities will start showing up. The alternative? Doing nothing. Not doing what I love. Not pushing forward to get better. And, more than likely, not getting those same opportunities I will by sticking to my process.

Writing this book is a part of my pursuit. It's a part of my journey. Sure, I wish things may have happened faster, but they didn't. It's important to not get hung up on something not working out the way you wanted it to. The important thing is learning from your experiences. You learn, adjust, and keep moving forward.

Punt the Quitters Mentality

What if you were right there before your goal and quit? You must eradicate the *Quitters Mentality.* Don't even entertain the possibility of quitting. In your mind, you need to know that you're going all the way, no matter what. Keep trying different variables to see what the winning formula is. Every rep will give you one more layer of confidence. Consistency comes from the reps.

Sure, I get mad when things don't work. I can get pissed and frustrated just like everyone else, but you can't let that deter you. That's when self-confidence enters the picture. I tell myself, "G, you're close. You're almost there. Keep going." Maybe there's one variable that you haven't figured out all the way yet. Maybe you ran into an unexpected obstacle.

Whatever the case, my confidence kicks in because I know I'm going to figure out how to make it work.

Master Your Craft

In order to truly master your craft, you need to dial into the process. Be a student of your game. Education and practical application will produce the confidence you need. I'm talking about completely immersing yourself with your craft, one million percent. Many people think they are fully immersing themselves, but they miss the mark and aren't actually fully all-in. To have the chance or opportunity to make something successful is extremely difficult. You have to make sure your level of commitment in the real world actually matches what you think it is in your head.

So, how can you experience something like that? How can you get to that next level? A giant piece of the puzzle is *bulletproofing your confidence* to the point where you refuse to give up, no matter what. It's getting to a level of self-belief that no matter the obstacle, your viewpoint is that you're going to figure it out.

People give up too easily. When people get hit with the slightest bit of resistance, they want to give up, and there's never a shortage of excuses. There will always be people who say,

"Well, that's pretty risky." People will absolutely doubt you, and that's okay. I told you that it was going to be tough." That's the naysayer bullshit.

You can't throw in the towel so easily. They're saying these things to you because of their own lack of confidence and because your pursuit of greatness makes them uncomfortable. Don't give in to this. Stick to your path, build your confidence, and make it happen for yourself.

This Book

Whether it's an opinion held by one person or an opinion shared by 20, it doesn't matter. That applies to this book as well. Maybe people will love it. Maybe they won't. Maybe it will be a bestseller. Maybe, I won't sell it at all. Hell, maybe I have to give it away.

I don't know yet, and that's okay. I'm confident that I will figure it out.

Most things in life don't work the first time. I would argue that they're not supposed to, and I'll tell you why. If everything always worked out on the first try, what good is that going to do? What will you learn with there never being any barriers or obstacles standing between you and your goal? You'll think that everything is easy and never learn the value of hard work and perseverance.

Instead, reframe it in your mind. Start to look at obstacles differently. Conquering each obstacle is bringing you one step closer. God is trying to tell me, show me, and challenge me. It's a test of how bad I want it - how bad you want it. How hard are you willing to work for it?

Remember: I don't just *kind of* want it.

Winners Win

It can be greatly demoralizing when things don't work out the way you anticipated. You can visualize the outcome of situations a thousand times and still be disappointed by the results once it happens. I've been in situations where I've had to lick my wounds, just like everyone else. I've had my share of bad days and weeks.

But you know what? I'm still betting on myself. I'm still going to bet on my team to figure things out. Instead of focusing on the failure, I start looking to the next thing and knowing that if I keep down this path, I will be successful eventually. That's confidence.

When you can start to build confidence around self-reliance and knowing that you will get through it, you become unstoppable. You know that you are going to win, it's just a matter of time. This mindset is powerful and can get you through a lot of dark times and setbacks.

I say this definitively because I've already seen how true it is. If you accept this as your truth, then part of that is putting your vibe out there into the universe. It's just how it works. The phrase *"Winners Win"* rings true. That winning mentality starts from within.

Just because something doesn't work out doesn't mean that it's a loss. It just means that you need to try something else. *Just don't give up. Don't be afraid to change.* If something doesn't work, then zoom out to analyze what happened. Have you been putting enough time into the project? Have you been consistent? Have you been putting in enough effort and focus?

What variables do you control that you can change? More than likely, you'll be able to figure out how to make it work when you step back and analyze it like this.

Don't Give Up On What You Want

The bottom line of this book and of my life: *don't give up on what you want*. Adapting, rolling with the punches, and being flexible are key components on the road to achievement. If you put in enough consistent reps, you'll start to believe and understand that things will eventually work out. You may be three feet or two-thousand feet from gold.

One of the questions I've been asked frequently is, "G, if you knew how long it was going to take, how hard it was going to be, would you sign up to do it again?" The answer to this question is a resounding "Yes" because my life is mine. I created it for myself, and I never threw the towel in when I got punched in the face with adversity.

My entire lifestyle has been built on developing *true confidence,* not some fabricated fake-ass confidence. True, genuine confidence is built through *education*. It's built through *practical application*. It's built through being *solutions-based and figuring shit out as you go.* You're not going to have all the answers on day one, but if you apply and execute the principles in this book, then you'll eventually figure it out.

Believe in Where You Want to Go

As you finish this book, remember to trust in the process as you embark on your journey. Show up every day and put in the work required. You're going to experience the entire spectrum of highs and lows, and you should start this process with that in mind. I'm not going to sugarcoat it, not every situation is going to be fun or pleasant. Things *will* suck sometimes. Knowing this, accepting it, and using it to your advantage mentally will help you build that confidence.

Dive head-first into the fire when things suck. *Embrace it.* Taking on hard shit head-on is where the sauce is. That's when you see what you're truly made of. You deal with the obstacle, figure out the best course of action, then move on. Every time you conquer an obstacle, it's another vote of confidence gained towards your mission.

It's a Long Game

I've been in the game for 20 plus years. That's a long time. A lot of people don't want to sign up for that, and I get it. But if I had to do it all over again I would, no questions asked. My life is mine; it's not boring, and things are interesting even when things don't work out the way I want them to.

It's a fucking challenge. When I find the winning solution, my confidence levels up even more. How could you not believe in yourself if you consistently prove that you can get through whatever is thrown your way?

So, next time you come up against something that doesn't work, don't be too hard on yourself. Evaluate what went wrong and come up with a new strategy. Don't give up until you find the winning formula. Doing so will add fuel to your fire of confidence.

CHAPTER SEVEN

WIN AT LIFE

Y OU'VE HEARD THE stories of hardship. You've heard the stories of victory. You've heard the stories of putting in the work required.

You've started to understand the possibilities that are available.

But the million-dollar question is: How do you tie it all together?

How can you apply these principles to take action in your life *today?*

I shared these experiences and stories with you because I want you to *understand* what it really took for me to get here. A linear path to success and confidence doesn't exist. You're going to have your ups, downs, and flat lines - it's inevitable. Things almost never work out on the timeline you laid out. Life just doesn't work that way.

However, as I've shown you in this book, it's all possible if you keep showing up and keep putting in the work. Life and success are the sum of your daily actions, and that's what I want you to take away from this book.

In this final chapter, I'll give you actionable steps to write down your goals, your plan of action, and finally, your plan to go execute and win at life.

The Way Out

For me, all I knew was that I needed to get out of the coal mine. I knew that on my first day working 600 feet underground. Upon accepting the job, I knew immediately that I had a purpose, a timeframe, and a way out.

The way in was the way out.

Similarly, I recognized the opportunity the first time I set foot on the campus of Columbus State to learn what I wanted to do. I began to understand what was possible when someone paid me $20 for my first personal training session.

Those were my *entry points.*

This was the start of my process to start *winning in life.*

Still, I had demons to battle. I had things to work through, and it was far from smooth sailing.

What does your path look like? What's your version of this book? How can you apply what you've learned through these pages and stories?

And finally, where do you start?

#1 What is your definitive purpose?

To get started, you need to ask yourself some questions.

- What is your definitive purpose?

- What is your driving force?

- What is the thing that on your worst day will make you persevere?

- What is it that makes your life worth living?

- What do you want to accomplish in your lifetime?

- What do you want to be known for?

I was able to make that kind of change. I was able to create that type of life. I was able to answer those questions and apply the answers to create success and confidence. Now, how do you do the same in your own life?

What's your version?
Personally, I wanted to change past, current, and future generations of Gregory's from what I would go on to accomplish. I wanted to blaze a path to open new opportunities for my family that would create long-lasting positive change.

What is that for you?
Maybe it's the same thing; maybe it's not. Regardless, you must identify your version. Some people reference it as their *why*. Pinpointing your purpose is of the utmost importance because you are always going to have to rely on it.

It's okay if you aren't quite sure. But just know that *it is* inside of you. I can't give it to you. Your mom or dad can't give it to you. Your friends can't give it to you. Hell, not even your enemies can give it to you. It has to be yours, and it has to come from within.

What is going to keep you awake at night because you want it so bad? What is going to light the wick that can't go out? My wick doesn't go out. It's lit and always burning strong.

Finding your purpose - finding your why - changes everything.

ACTION STEP:

Write down your definitive purpose. *In your own words in the space below, right down your why. Then, keep this book and refer back to the answers you write down in the pages to come. Rely on this guide and what you write down when you need to be reminded why you're doing all the things you need to do to be successful.*

_____

_____

_____

_____

_____

_____

_____

_____

_____

_____

_____

_____

_____

#2 What does your best day look like?

- What is your best day?

- What is your best life?

- When are you your happiest?

That's the reason you want to change, right? You want to change to create that best day; that best life; that sustained happiness.

That's why you wrote down your why above. That's why you're reading this book. But, how do you get to that point?

Here's another way to think about it:

What would you do every day to fulfill your purpose if you had an unlimited amount of money?

You may think, "G, that's easy for you to say because you have fitness as your job, and you've had this success." Remember, I didn't know a single person that was a personal trainer. I had zero contacts. There was no internet, no one to mentor me, and no blueprint. Being a personal trainer didn't exist in the Ohio Valley when I was coming up.

I created my own blueprint. For a while, I was my own mentor. I relied on the library, magazines, and everything I could get my hands on before the internet rolled around.

Longaberger Baskets

There's a company east of Columbus called Longaberger Baskets. The founder, Dave Longaberger, made millions of dollars from selling handwoven baskets. He literally built a five-story basket as his corporate headquarters.

Do you think people thought he was crazy when he told them that he wanted to sell baskets? Of course, but it didn't matter. It didn't matter because that's what he wanted to do.

Just like I wanted to lift weights and get paid. Now, you need to start writing down your passions so that you can structure your life in a way to build around them.

ACTION STEP:

What is your passion? What are you going to build in order to realize your purpose? *Using the space below, list out your number one passion in life. Then, write down at least three steps you can take each day to build a life around that passion.*

_____

_____

_____

_____

_____

#3 What is the lifestyle that you want to live?

- What's your ideal lifestyle look like?

- Where do you want to live?

- What kind of cars do you want to drive?

- What kind of house do you want to live in?

- What type of people do you want to have around you?

Don't gloss over this. Visualizing the lifestyle you seek is important. I put together my first vision board when I was just 20 years old. And guess what? I'm living in a house that almost looks exactly like the picture on my board. Think of this as another way of writing down goals. You're writing down the life you want to live, and you're doing it in a way that reminds you of your why every damn day.

There is great power in the practice of visualization. Harnessing this power relies on clearly defining your goals. Left undefined, you become a drifter.

I never thought I would own a Rolls-Royce, but I do.

I never thought I would own a Presidential Rolex, but I do.

No lie, these are all things I saw in the rap videos. For me, material possessions are not the end point. Material items are items that allow me to continue to push. It's a different level of expectation I demand of myself. It's not about a thing. It's about a purpose. It's about an expectation.

- What is my driving purpose?

- What is my passion?

- What do I want to do every day?

ACTION STEP:

Now, build and shape your goals around the lifestyle you seek. *Write down 3-5 goals below.*

1.

2.

3.

4.

5.

#4 Non-negotiable habits

- What are you willing to do for it?

- What processes are you going to put in place?

- What time will you get up every day?

- What type of material do you need to study to be able to do your passion?

- What books do you need to read?

- What mentors do you need to seek out?

- Who do you need to understand?

- Who do you need to listen to?

I'm talking about *total immersion*.

ACTION STEP:

Based on the questions above, write down your game plan to execute on the goals you previously listed.

_____

_____

_____

_____

_____

_____

_____

_____

_____

_____

_____

_____

_____

Be Relentless

Clearly define your purpose, passion, lifestyle, and non-negotiable habits.

It's going to take time. But, in order to *Win at Life*, you have to show up every single day. It doesn't stop with the end goal. *Winning at Life* lies within the pursuit - within the journey.

What does this mean?

It means you need to pursue something that you want to learn about. To pursue something that will help someone. To pursue something that will positively impact your family.

Throughout this process, you're going to win some. You're going to lose some. You'll get knocked down, and you'll get back up. You'll battle, and you'll ultimately persevere.

That's the journey. *That's the sauce.*

Are you winning? *Winning is the expectation.*

There are levels to winning and levels to success. Not everyone's definition of success is the same. But, in my opinion, if you love what you do and are pursuing your best self, then you are winning.

Thank you for taking the time to read this book. I hope that I've provoked some thought, and I hope you are beginning to understand what's possible in this life.

I hope these words inspire you to begin to take charge.

I refuse to be the 100-year-old guy filled with regret. I know wholeheartedly that I won't regret rolling the dice to be the best me. I won't regret putting in the reps. I won't regret squeezing every ounce out of this body to give myself every opportunity to win in this life.

I want that for myself. I want that for my family, and I want that for you.

And, I want you to know that it's all possible if you take the steps necessary to build confidence and take action.

Thank you for reading my book. I know parts of it may sound crazy, but the reality is that I never wanted to be mediocre. I always wanted to be elite, and I will fight every day till the day I die to push myself to that level.

I hope you will join me in that battle. You won't regret it.

Cory Gregory
@corygfitness

Made in the USA
Monee, IL
11 May 2022

96235600R00075